BY THE
LOVE OF CHRIST

INTIMACY

CHALLENGES IN
COMPLETE OBEDIENCE

Becky Castle

ISBN-13:978-1727515275

ISBN-10:1727515277

CONTENTS

Challenge One	The Thirsting Soul	6
Challenge Two	Discerning the Voice of The Lord	13
Challenge Three	Knowing the Voice of God	21
Challenge Four	Praying in Agreement	27
Challenge Five	The Table of Intimacy	34
Challenge Six	The Value of Risk	41
Challenge Seven	The Seeds of Intimacy	49
Challenge Eight	The Strength of Praise and Worship	56
Challenge Nine	Glory in the Sufferings	62
Challenge Ten	Loyalty in the Kingdom	70

PRINCIPLES OF CAPTIVATED BY THE LOVE OF CHRIST

CHALLENGE ONE

Encountering God's presence is the only satisfying source of life that reaches the depths of our hearts.

CHALLENGE TWO

Spiritual maturity requires the ability to discern God's voice from Satan's and our own imaginations.

CHALLENGE THREE

It is not enough to discern God's voice...you must obey Him.

CHALLENGE FOUR

The prayer of Faith drives us to dependency and intimacy with God.

CHALLENGE FIVE

Time alone with God in the Word and with prayer *is* the table for intimacy.

CHALLENGE SIX

Personal value in Christ is affirmed when we take risks of Faith and Belief in the Kingdom of God.

CHALLENGE SEVEN

Faith matures only when we exercise it, by believing in a Sovereign God.

CHALLENGE EIGHT

True praise and worship strengthens the spirit and delivers the believer from waywardness.

CHALLENGE NINE

Obedience to God is perfected in the midst of sufferings.

CHALLENGE TEN

Godly loyalty to another reflects one's intimate commitment to Christ.

CHALLENGE ONE

THE THIRSTING SOUL

"As the deer pants for water brooks, so my soul pants for Thee, O God. My soul thirsts for God, for the living God."

Psalm 42:1-2

Focusing Your Heart

I rush to the water's edge, seeking Your presence. I long to be fully satisfied, consumed by Your Love. Take me deeper into Your refreshing, life-giving presence.

Fixing Your Mind

Christ is never where He cannot be found. He is not too far away. He is near, able, and willing to fulfill the intimate longings of the heart, mind, and soul.

FULFILLING HIS WILL

A. The Thirsting Soul

Imagine the deer of Psalm 42. He has been thirsting for water for days, searching for a flowing stream. His thirst deepens and he pants, longing to quench his thirst. Have you ever experienced this thirsting in your life? Does your soul long for more, yet you are weary from searching in unsatisfying places?

How does David compare the body to the spirit in Psalm 63:1?

_____

_____

_____

Many times, the Word likens the body's thirst for water to the spirit's craving for the Lord's Presence.

What circumstances caused David to thirst?

_____

_____

_____

The Psalmist hasn't been able to find water, and these circumstances have caused him to feel dry and weary. Is there a besetting sin, or feelings of aimlessness or loneliness? Are you harboring bitterness, or living in rebellion? In the natural realm, the first step to emotional or physical healing is to acknowledge those needs *you* cannot meet. The same principle exists in the spiritual realm.

The first step to having your needs met is to identify them. Ask the Lord to reveal your needs as you remain silent before Him. Write down what you hear. Be specific and honest as to what your heart is telling you.

_____

_____

_____

Psalms chapters 42 and 63 describe David's desperate longings to see the Lord. He also describes in detail the pain his sin has caused him. Can you relate with these feelings? (Read Psalm 32:3-4).

B. The Source of Satisfaction

Once our needs have been made bare, we make room in our hearts for them to be healed. Ezekiel was a prophet who identified the source from which all things can be satisfied (See Ezekiel 47:1-12). The water in this passage gives life. In verse 8, the river flows into the Arabah, which is now known as the Red Sea. What happens to the Dead Sea when it encounters this river?

_____
_____
_____

That sea that was once full of death has come to life. What causes the change?

_____
_____

What is needed in our lives for change to occur?

_____
_____
_____

God alone is the Source of healing. As we meet with God, the power of His Life replaces the dead, sinful, and fleshly patterns of our thinking and old way of living.

In order to fully understand the powers of the waters, we must determine its source. Ezekiel sees the water coming from under the threshold of the temple (Ezekiel 47:1). Apostle John experienced a similar vision in Revelation 22:1. Describe the river and its source.

_____

_____

_____

The Lord God Almighty is the only Hope for an unexplainable life. All our needs can be met, and every desire fulfilled by Him. Fill in the charts below.

Psalm 145:18-19 Need	2 Corinthians 12:7-10 Need	Matthew 8:2-3 Need
Fulfillment	Fulfillment	Fulfillment
Source	Source	Source

The elements of faith and belief bring us to the threshold of God's presence, where every desire, weakness, and sin can find fulfillment, strength, and cleansing in Him.

C. An Invitation to the Water's Edge

In Isaiah 55:1-3, an invitation is extended to those who hunger and thirst. How does this passage relate to you personally?

_____

_____

_____

God calls us to come to Him and drink His waters. We do not have to earn the privilege. He longs to satisfy the cravings of our souls.

What does Jesus say in John 4:13-14 about the quality of the water He gives?

_____

Jesus is completely capable and willing to quench our thirst. His satisfaction is unceasing, perpetually satisfying; causing us to be "like a watered garden, and like a spring of water, whose waters do not fail" (Isaiah 58:11).

In Psalm 63, God does not satisfy our hungering with limited nourishment. How does He feed us?

_____

_____

How can we plant ourselves by the Source?

1. _____
2. _____
3. _____

The Lord feeds us with the "richest of foods", with marrow and fatness.

Firmly planting ourselves near the Source will allow us to continuously receive the nourishment for which we hunger and thirst – the life our soul craves.

We must turn from the way of the wicked and choose to delight in the principles of God's Word day and night. Meditation on the Word, along with prayer, allows our spiritual needs to encounter the only Source who can fulfill our desires with unfailing satisfaction.

"Come to me all who are weary and heavy laden, and I will give you rest. Take My yoke upon you, and learn from Me, for I am gentle and humble in heart; and you shall find rest for your souls. For My yoke is easy and My load is light" (Matthew 11:28-30).

COMPLETING OBEDIENCE

1) Principle: Encountering God's presence is the only satisfying Source of life that reaches the depths of our heart.

2) Are there any sins, influences, or circumstances barring you from the threshold of God's presence?

3) Read Matthew 11:28-30. The need to come to the water's edge is necessary to encounter God's presence. God always allows us to be needy. Only then will we come to Him in brokenness and humility. What is the need of your life or heart today?

4) Memorize Psalm 42:1-2.

CHALLENGE TWO

DISCERNING THE VOICE OF THE LORD

"...he who is spiritual appraises all things..."
1 Corinthians 2:15

Focusing Your Heart

Your Word commands me to cry out for wisdom and discernment. Teach me to discern Your voice from the deceptive voices of the enemy. Your voice is the one I desire to recognize and follow.

Fixing Your Mind

The new man in Christ no longer desires fellowship with the enemy and the world. We long to discern the difference from those voices we have known in the past, and the one we now belong to and love. God's voice is distinctly different from the one who kills, steals, and destroys in our life. Upon learning to identify and respond to the voice of God as He intimately speaks to us, we will not fall into temptation.

FULLING HIS WILL

A. Deceptive Voices

1. List the way the enemy destroys life:

John 8:44

_____

John 10:10, 12-13

_____

1 Peter 5:8

_____

Revelation 12:9

_____

Revelation 12:10

_____

The enemy is a liar, thief, murderer, deceiver, and accuser. He is a trespasser, forcing his way into our mind, will, and emotions. Are there areas in your life that you have yielded to the enemy's deception? How did this come about?

_____

_____

How can you overcome this failure? (Colossians 3:5-10)

_____

_____

2. Read James 3:14-16 and 1 John 2:15-17. Describe the world's voice.

_____

_____

Selfishness is the core of worldly characters. When you are seeking answers about a situation in your life, you must choose to hear God's voice above the voice of the world and our own imagination.

3. Read Romans 8:5-8, and Galatians 5: 19-21. How is the self-life or flesh portrayed?

_____

_____

The flesh always sets itself against the spirit. They are in direct opposition. One area that plagues man is in the imagination. We are to test every thought against the knowledge of God (See 2 Corinthians 10:5). The knowledge of God is the Word of God by which we test every spirit (1 John 4:1-6). You will commonly find yourself unwilling to seek or listen to God about your circumstances. Choosing to accept fleshly thoughts will cause you to set other priorities above hearing God's voice. What is the result of heeding the voice of the enemy, the world, or the flesh? (James 1:13-16)

_____

_____

Barriers between you, God, and others will occur every time you are deceived. Obeying the voice of the devil, the world, or your flesh, will damage your intimacy with God.

B. Hearing God's Voice

Characterize the sound of God's voice (Matthew 10:20; Galatians 5:22-23).

_____

_____

_____

God always speaks within the realm of His nature. He speaks to His children patiently, peacefully, lovingly, and with joy, goodness, and self-control. His communication with us will produce fruit in our life that is consistent with His character.

Read Song of Solomon 2:7-10, 3:1-5.

The Lover, representing Jesus, is pursuing His bride, the Church. What does the Lover earnestly urge the daughters of Jerusalem to do concerning the one He loves? (2:7)

_____

_____

Earlier in Song of Solomon, the Lover has called His bride. Now, He waits for her to desire Him. How does she respond? (vs 8-9)

_____

_____

_____

What is the next call of the Lover? (vs 10)

_____

_____

What is the sequence of events in their relationship?
(3:1-5)

_____

_____

The bride is excited about Christ pursuing her. She
responds with joy and anticipation. He calls her to come
and follow Him. There are times in our walk with God
when we do not hear His voice. He is quiet and not to be
found. In these moments, we must guard our hearts from
deceptive voices. What did the bride do? (vs 2-4)

_____

How does Psalm 27:14 instruct us to deal with times of
silence?

_____

_____

What should be the confidence of our heart? (Jeremiah
29:12-13)

_____

_____

The bride sought her Lover until she found Him. She did
not make decisions apart from waiting for a word from
Him. Waiting upon the Lord produced in her a holy

Character reflecting the beauty of the One she loved
(Song of Solomon 4).

During these waiting periods, certain principles are to be
applied. What are they?

1. Psalm 46:10

_____

2. Proverbs 3:5-6

_____

C. Distraction from His Voice

Read Luke 10:38-42

Contrast the different attitudes and behaviors of Mary
and Martha toward Jesus.

_____

_____

What was Jesus's response to Martha's complaint? (vs
41-42)

_____

_____

What distractions are keeping you from hearing the
voice of the Lord?

_____

_____

The most important thing Mary could do was to listen to her Lord. What was it that compelled her to forsake the cares of her life in order to sit at Jesus's feet and listen to His every word?

_____

_____

Mary believed Jesus's word to be the Words of God. When Jesus confronted Peter's allegiance, how did he respond? (John 6:66-68)

_____

_____

We must decide that the voice of the Lord is absolutely vital for life. Desiring to hear His voice, and His alone, will sensitize us to the loud, deceiving voices of the enemy, the world, and our flesh. Those voices may seem pleasurable for a time, but they will always bring destruction. God's voice, when we hear and obey, will always bring life and peace.

COMPLETING OBEDIENCE

1) Principle: Spiritual maturity requires the ability to discern God's voice from Satan's and our own imaginations.

2) Write down everything that "speaks" into your life. Honestly evaluate whether or not the influences in your life are consistent with the character of God.

3) Repent of those influences that hinder God's voice in your life daily. Begin crying out to God for a discerning spirit to be developed within you.

4) Memorize 1 Corinthians 2:15.

KNOWING THE VOICE OF GOD

"My sheep hear my voice, and I know them, and they follow me."

John 10:27

Focusing Your Heart

Father, Your word teaches that a believer can know Your voice. I am Your child. Enable me to become sensitive to the sound of Your voice, and immediately draw near when you call.

Fixing Your Mind

God loves His creation – **you**! He wants to know you and be known by you. The Scriptures parallel our relationship with God to the intimacy of a shepherd and his sheep. The relationship is one of great dependency. As a part of His flock, we, the sheep, are to be trained to respond only to the Shepherd's voice. Our obedience will lead us beside still waters, along the paths of righteousness and protect us even in the midst of trouble.

FULFILLING HIS WILL

A. Knowing the Voice of God

How do the Shepherd and His sheep recognize each other? (John 10:105, 27)

_____

_____

We can experience God authentically by honestly communicating and knowing the heart of the Lord as He speaks to us.

Read Psalm 139:1-18. Summarize God's "knowing" you.

_____

_____

_____

The Lord of all the earth is intimately acquainted with you. He knows everything about you. He carefully and specifically fashioned you in His image. His thoughts toward you are all-consuming, outnumbering the grains of sand.

In the Old and New Testaments, we find many illustrations of God speaking to His children. Read Joshua 8:1-30. How did Joshua know what to do when conquering Ai? (v. 1-2)

_____

_____

The Lord spoke to Joshua and gave him specific
instructions. The Israelites carried out God's instructions
and were victorious. Jesus wanted to let the church know
that He would always speak with them. God has enabled
us to hear His voice in order for us to know His heart.
He longs to share it with His children. The Lord has
valuable truth to teach believers. What does He
emphasize to the seven churches? (Revelation 2:1, 11,
17, 29; 3:6, 13, 22)

_____

_____

What does Jesus say about those who are intimate with
Him? (Luke 8:21)

_____

_____

To grow in intimacy with Jesus, we must not only know
the sound of His voice, but learn to sincerely hear and
obey Him.

B. The Intimacy of Hearing the Voice of God

There is a difference in physically hearing someone
speak and spiritually hearing from the heart. When Jesus
admonished the churches saying, "He who has ears to
hear, let them hear", He meant for them to respond with
their hearts. Why does Paul say that hearing the Word is
necessary for faith to grow? (Romans 10:17)

_____

_____

The Greek verb tense for hearing is continuous action.
The Word means the 'revealed Word,' or 'understood

Word'. To be intimate with Jesus means continuously hearing with our whole being so understanding will come.

Read Luke 10:38-42. What one thing did Jesus affirm about Mary?

_____

_____

When Jesus confronted Peter with a similar voice, how did Peter respond? (John 6:66-68)

_____

_____

Mary chose to make hearing from the Lord top priority. She could have been doing other things like Martha, but in her heart, nothing compared to hearing the voice of her Master. Likewise, Peter found life in the voice of the Lord. He determined that hearing His voice was the only thing that really mattered. By following His voice, he too, would experience a supernatural life.

C. The Intimacy of Doing the Will of God

Intimacy with Christ does not occur only by knowing and hearing His voice. It is built upon possessing and sharing His purpose and life in the Kingdom of God.

How is intimacy with God portrayed in Matthew 22:37?

_____

We are to love God with all that is in us. We cannot separate physically hearing and knowing God's voice from willfully obeying it, and think we can be intimate with Him.

Read James 1:22-25. How does God describe one who is intimate with Him?

_____

_____

What compels God to reveal Himself? (John 14:21)

_____

_____

Why does obedience open the way to intimacy? (Psalm 25:14; James 2:20-26)

_____

_____

Obedience demonstrates faith. It seals in the heart and will what the mind claims to know and believe.

Read John 13:1-17. Give the life principle illustrated in this passage concerning responding to the voice of God.

_____

_____

Intimacy will be fulfilled as we learn to know, hear, and then obey His voice. An obedient life will build a secure foundation in our walk with the Lord. What is the result in the life of one who obeys the voice of God? (Matthew 7:24-27)

_____

_____

COMPLETING OBEDIENCE

1) Principle: It is not enough to discern God's voice – you must obey Him.

2) Set aside time to listen to God's voice. Write down what you hear. It may be His affirmation of love for you, direction for your day or life, or a truth to be applied. Test what you hear, and determine to obey God's voice.

3) Memorize John 10:5.

PRAYING IN AGREEMENT

"If you abide in Me and My words abide in you, ask whatever you wish, and it shall be done for you."

John 15:7

Focusing Your Heart

The truth is, Father, confidence is lacking in my prayer life. At times, I am unsure You hear me or answer me. Teach me to pray so my life touches Your heart and impacts the world.

Fixing Your Mind

God is looking for believers who will know His heart, join with Him, and bring His Kingdom on earth as it is in heaven (Isaiah 59:16). It is time for those who desire intimacy with the Lord to pick up the mantle of prayer. Through open and honest prayer, our faith in Him to affect our lives, our families, and even whole nations will consume our hearts.

FULFILLING HIS WILL

A. God Is Looking Throughout the Earth

Read Isaiah 59:16, and Ezekiel 22:30. What is God looking for?

_____

_____

Why?

_____

_____

Describe the person for whom God is searching (Psalm 24:3-6; 2 Chronicles 16:9).

_____

_____

_____

What happens when a righteous man or woman prays? (James 5:16-18)

_____

_____

What was the result of Elijah's praying?

_____

_____

Define "Intercessor".

_____

_____

The redemption of man is the passion of God's heart. Everything He does centers around restoring His bride back to intimacy with Him. He has chosen to work out

28

redemption through the faith and obedience of His church through His son. Choosing to passionately pray in faith and belief and joining His call of restoration is not optional. The prayer and intercession of the righteous releases God's power for life transformation in us, and those who God places on our hearts. Prayer, as intercession, is standing in the gap. Standing in the gap is strategic intervention. Such action is believing for one who is unable to believe God for himself.

B. Moving Mountains

You may be thinking, "I am not Elijah. I do not have mighty faith." Read James 5:17 again. How does it describe Elijah?

In his humanity, there was nothing extraordinary about him. What made the difference?

What makes a man righteous in God's sight?

Give the promise in each of the following verses for those who believe in God:

1. Jeremiah 33:32

2. Matthew 21:21-22

3. John 15:7

_____

4. Hebrews 4:16

_____

5. 1 John 5:14-15

_____

In these verses, what are the limits to the requests?

_____

God responds mightily and swiftly to those who pray in faith. We can ask in faith when we ask according to His heart and Word. As we come to know God and His Word, we become confident we will receive our requests. God will move mountains of bitterness, insecurity, and strife, and affect continents on behalf of situations when praying in agreement with Him. You have His Promise!

C. The Spiritual Birthing Process

Think about the process of physically conceiving a child. Did you know the scriptures often compare God's work to birthing a child? Write down some ways you think they relate:

_____
_____
_____

Conception takes place only after a man and a woman have united themselves physically. For nine months, the child is nurtured and matures until time for birth. The labor process brings much travail and sacrifice. Comparatively, the Word of God enters your life as a seed, maturing Christ's characters and purposes in time. What is necessary for two to walk in unity? (Amos 3:3; 2 Corinthians 6:16)

_____

_____

What then unites the believer with God in prayer?

_____

How does agreement with God affect prayer? (John 16:23-24; Matthew 18:19)

_____

Read Isaiah 66:7-9. When does the birth take place? (v. 7) _____

When our heart is in agreement with God in prayer, conception in the spiritual realm takes place. We may not see the answer immediately, but it is the joining of wills that sets things in motion (Hebrews 11:1; 2 Corinthians 4:18). How does Paul describe his relationship to the believers in Galatians 4:19?

_____

_____

It often takes a laboring process to produce a thing of value. Most of us get discouraged and disappointed when we don't see immediate results after praying. We must remember that it takes time to birth a child. And in between, there is pain and joy, discomfort and satisfaction, incredible love, bonding, and intimacy.

Read Mark 5:27-30. What was the woman's cry?

_____

How was Jesus aware of His need to respond?

_____

Agreement with God's heart and travailing in the prayer of faith is the price to pay in knowing God. Like the woman in Mark 5, this touches God, releasing His power – someone is born again, another healed, a marriage holds together, and a nation is changed. This is the unexplainable, intimate life.

COMPLETING OBEDIENCE

1) Principle: The prayer of faith drives us to dependency and intimacy with God.

2) Who, in your life, needs your prayerful, strategic intervention? Begin standing in the gap on their behalf.

3) What situation have you ceased praying over? Return to believing God in prayer.

4) Memorize Ezekiel 22:30.

CHALLENGE FIVE

THE TABLE OF INTIMACY

"He has brought me to his banquet hall, and his banner over me is love."

Song of Solomon 2:4

Focusing Your Heart

Thank You for seating me at Your table. I know the King always provides the best for His servants. Strengthen me with the meat of Your Word. Fill me from the fountain of living waters.

Fixing Your Mind

The table is the place of God's presence and provision. When we come to the table, we expose ourselves to all that God is. However, to become like Him, we must partake at the table daily.

FULFILLING HIS WILL

A. Face-to-Face with Almighty God

The tabernacle in the Old Testament was the place for meeting with God. Every article in the tabernacle represents different aspects of our relationship with Him.

What did the table of shewbread represent? (Exodus 25:23-30)

_____

Jamieson, Fausset, and Brown, in their *Commentary on the Whole Bible,* say the bread symbolizes "the full and never-failing provision that is made in the church for the spiritual sustenance and refreshment of God's people."

Read John 6:32-35; 41-58. Who is the true bread for us now? (v. 55-57)

_____

How do we "partake of His flesh"?

_____

_____

In the Old Testament, the table of shewbread symbolized the presence of God. Now Jesus embodies the presence, and we learn to partake of the life of Christ through faith. Coming to the table allows us to partake of the Living Word of God that is in Christ. The life of Christ in us reveals the written Word to us (2 Peter 1:20-21).

How is the written Word revealed to us?

2 Timothy 3:16

_____

_____

Hebrews 4:12

_____

_____

John 17:17

_____

_____

Read Hebrews 5:11-14. What two examples of food are used, and how are they related to the levels of intimacy we have with God?

1. _____

2. _____

What should be the outcome of one who eats solid food? (v. 13-14)

_____

_____

_____

When we first come to Christ, we are immature. We cannot digest the deeper truths of the Christian life until we lay the foundation of the basics (Hebrews 6:1-2). As we mature in our faith and belief, the exchanged life with Christ gives spiritual discernment to understand the teaching of righteousness.

B. Feasting on God's Word

Spiritual realities are eternal but often unseen. In contrast, temporal realities are always recognizable (2 Corinthians 4:18).

We spend so much time eating physical food to sustain us. How much more should we take care of our spiritual needs? How did Jeremiah and Job feel, and respond to the words of God? (Jeremiah 15:16; Job 23:12)

_____

_____

How do we internalize God's Word into our mind and emotions? How will it become the delight of our heart and more necessary than our physical food? In each of the following verses, discover and write down ways you can allow God's Word to penetrate your heart.

1)   Matthew 11:15; Luke 11:28; Romans 10:17

_____

_____

_____

Hearing God's Word with not only our ears but also with our heart is the first step of faith to be awakened in us. We must hear the Word if we are to believe (Romans 10:14).

2)   Psalm 119:9,11; Proverbs 3:1-3

_____

_____

_____

Binding the Word to our heart by memorize it will guard us from sin.

3)   2 Timothy 2:15; Acts 17:11; Psalm 1:2-3

_____

_____

Searching in the Word on a deeper level reveals life principles that will shape our hearts before the Lord.

4) John 4:34; James 1:22-25

_____

_____

Our level of commitment in obeying His Word parallels our desire for intimacy with Him. Reading, studying, memorizing, and meditating on God's Word provides the right environment to ask the question, "How would God have me respond?"

C. Internalizing the Word of Truth

Read Joshua 24:14-15. How do you serve God "wholeheartedly"?

_____

There will be the need to alter your lifestyle to make room for this intimate relationship. Coming to the table of God's presence will cause further changes as you yield your rights to Him.

How does Jesus challenge those who desire to follow Him? (Matthew 5:20; 8:18-22)

_____

Jesus spoke of this heart relationship, "Unless your righteousness surpasses that of the scribes and Pharisees, you shall not see the kingdom of heaven" (Matthew 5:20). Legalism is striving to achieve godliness in the flesh. The opposite extreme is to do nothing. These temptations to ritualize, or avoid daily experience with God, will leave you empty and shallow.

How do you internalize the truth in your daily experience with God? A teachable heart makes the way for true life in one's relationship with God. The following are ways to keep your heart open to the Lord:

1) Read Psalm 119:162-168. What is the psalmist's perspective?

_____

Spending time alone with God in His Word builds truth and righteousness into the mind, will, and emotions.

2) Read Proverbs 3:1-3. What are we to write?

_____
_____

Journaling can help the truth become written in your heart. Writing out your prayers, thoughts, and specific insights revealed to you by God helps internalize His character into your life.

3) Read Mark 1:35. What did Jesus do on a regular basis?

_____

Drawing aside consistently with God is foundational to a trusting relationship.

COMPLETING OBEDIENCE

1) Principle: Time alone with God in the Word with prayer is the table for intimacy.

2) Choose a time, place, and a plan to begin building your time alone with God each day.

3) Review the principles of "internalizing" God's Word to help you begin your journey.

4) Memorize Acts 17:11

THE VALUE OF RISK

"....What is that to you? You follow Me!"

John 21:22

Focusing Your Heart

Father, I honestly fear following You at times. The Scriptures reveal that Your love drives out fear. Strengthen Your love in my heart to overcome the paralyzed feelings of fear.

Fixing Your Mind

God's strength is perfected in our willingness to submit our weaknesses to Him. Exposure of our frailties is a risk when seeking intimacy with God.

FULFILLING HIS WILL

A. His Strength Perfecting Our Weakness

Read Matthew 5:1-11.

What was the relationship between Peter and Jesus? (v. 5)

_____

_____

How do you think Peter, a fisherman by trade, felt when Jesus told him to put his net out for a catch?

_____

_____

If you were Peter, would you have responded in the same way? When the nets were filled, what were the reactions of Peter and his companions? (v. 8-10)

_____

_____

What emotion did Jesus uncover in Peter? (v. 10)

_____

He had come face to face with Christ the Lord, and his total humanity was revealed. To walk with Jesus means that our humanity, flesh, and sin will be confronted by the purity and truth of Almighty God. Intimacy requires vulnerability—a willingness to continue on in the relationship when faced with conflict.

How did Jesus address the reactions of the fisherman? (v.10)

_____

_____

He did not ridicule or preach at them. He spoke to their need and to their fear, then boldly proclaimed what He saw to be true by the Spirit instead of what He saw in their flesh. This is the way of intimacy with God—His strength perfecting our weakness. Do not be afraid. He loves to love you right where you are.

Read Matthew 26:69-75. Peter was constantly revealing the weakness of his flesh in the presence of his Master. How would you have felt if you had denied Jesus three times?

_____

_____

Peter wept bitterly. Shame and guilt flooded his heart. Peter became a changed man.

Read Psalm 34:18 and Proverbs 24:16. What brought about the difference in Peter's life?

_____

_____

_____

Peter exposed his weaknesses to the perfecting strength of his Savior. Are there any weaknesses you need to honestly expose to God?

B. Learning To Stand Alone

In Matthew chapter 15, the disciples witnessed Jesus feeding the multitude, healing the Canaanite woman's daughter, and casting out demons. Then they witnessed the Pharisees question Jesus' Messiahship.

Read Matthew 16:13-20. What did Jesus ask the disciples? (v. 13)

_____

_____

How did they respond? (v. 14)

_____

_____

Why did they respond incorrectly?

_____

_____

The Pharisees, Sadducees, and other leaders treated Jesus with contempt, and most of the disciples held back their confession of faith because of fear.

When Jesus asks the question again, how does Peter answer? (v. 16)

_____

_____

What's the difference between Peter and the other disciples?

_____

_____

Peter risked his reputation with those to whom he was closest because of his commitment to follow Christ. Intimacy with Christ calls for a commitment that is willing to stand alone. We will not be popular with the world or the religious community for the choices and confessions we make, but we will know a depth of relationship with the Lord that the world cannot experience.

How did Jesus reply to Peter's confession? (v. 17-19)

_____

_____

What life principle is represented in this account of Peter's life? (James 4:6-10)

_____

_____

To walk with God, we must take risks this world cannot know. We must humble ourselves and be willing to stand alone. Then, He will exalt us in His time.

C. Accepting Our Role in the Kingdom

Read John 21:15-22. After Jesus questioned Peter concerning his love for his Master, He signified the kind of death Peter would experience. Having been admonished to "feed the sheep", he was told he would be killed at the hands of others.

What was Peter's reaction (v. 20-21)?

_____

_____

Peter drew the attention away from himself and put it on John: "What about him? If this will happen to me, what about this man?"

How did Jesus answer? (v. 22)

_____

_____

Inherent to intimacy is a uniqueness in everyone's relationship to God. Your intimacy with Christ will be specifically fashioned for your role in the kingdom. Competing for other roles in the kingdom will violate the plans and purposes of God for you and others.

Whose race are you to run? (Hebrews 12:1-2)

_____

What two things will be necessary to run your race successfully?

1)_____

2)_____

What entanglements do you most fear?

_____

_____

To run a good race, you need to know who you are in relationship to the race. Peter lost his identity, security, and confidence when he compared himself to another man: "What about John?" He was singled out by his Master in an intimate moment because of the value of his life. We get entangled by rejecting our responsibility or role in the kingdom.

How does God's army work in His kingdom? (Joel 2:7-8, 11)

_____

_____

Every child of God has a unique place of ministry in His kingdom. One position is of no greater importance than the other. How does God instruct us to consider the members of His body? (1 Corinthians 12: 12-30)

_____

_____

Our value is found in our relationship with Christ. Intimacy with Him sets you free to receive your place in His kingdom, to be who He made you to be, and to confidently run your race.

COMPLETING OBEDIENCE

1) Principle: Personal value in Christ is affirmed when we take risks of faith and belief in the kingdom of God.

2) "A righteous man falls seven times and rises again" (Proverbs 24:16). What areas of weakness do you need to receive God's strength in in order to go on with God's plan for your life?

3) Memorize Hebrews 12:1-2.

THE SEED OF INTIMACY

"The kingdom of God is like a man who casts seed upon the soil."

Mark 4:26

Focusing Your Heart

I see in Your Word that I am to walk by faith, and not by sight. I confess and repent of unbelief in my heart. Develop in me unwavering faith.

Fixing Your Mind

Without faith, it is impossible to please God. Everything in a believer's life is an issue of faith. We must believe God is willing and able to fulfill every word He has given to His children. Step out in faith. Sow the seed of God's Word in belief and wait expectantly for Him.

FULFILLING HIS WILL

A. The Hope of Faith

Read Romans 4:1-5, 13-25.

How is a believer reckoned righteous in the sight of God?

_____

What does it mean "to be reckoned righteous"?

_____
_____

Righteousness comes by faith in the blood of Jesus to cover, pay for, and cleanse from sin, and to hold one securely in His presence. To be reckoned righteous is to be counted right with God, holy and made clean before Him.

How did Abraham respond to God's promise concerning his fatherhood of many nations? (v. 17-21). Be specific.

_____
_____
_____

Define "hope against hope".

_____
_____
_____

The "Word of promise" God gave to Abraham appeared to be impossible in the natural realm. There was no hope of it coming to pass. However, God's economy of provision is in the spiritual realm, and nothing is impossible with God (Matthew 19:26). Abraham believed the Word of God: "he did not waver in unbelief, but grew strong in faith", being fully persuaded that God would perform His promise. This kind of faith creates a trust necessary for intimacy with the Father.

B. The Test of Faith

Read Mark 4:35-41. What were the disciples' reactions to the storm? (v. 38)

_____

_____

What did they discover about the Lord through their experience? (v. 41)

_____

_____

How was their question of faith brought out in the open?

_____

_____

The disciples, fearful and panic-stricken, were very uncomfortable because they were out of control and in need. Like the disciples, we may become fearful, panic-stricken, angry, insecure, or defensive when faced with a need. Trials in our life are the training ground of our faith. Learning to steadfastly believe in God's power, love, and authority in every circumstance will enable you to overcome the tests of life.

Read Job 1:13-2:10. God allowed Satan to test Job. He lost his children, livestock, servants, and was plagued in his own body. In the midst of these trials, what was the testimony of Job's life? (v. 20-22; 2:10)

_____

_____

What spiritual principle did Job live out, enabling him to continue honoring God? (v. 22)

_____

Faith is not faith if it is altered by circumstances. We believe because there is One who is **ABSOLUTELY FAITHFUL.** Job's faith was in a sovereign God who, contrary to man, is never out of control, but whose righteousness prevails in all things (Isaiah 41:9-10).

C. Faith's Harvest

Read Mark 4:26-32, 11:22-25; 2 Corinthians 9:6, 8-15; and Galatians 6:7-9. What eternal principle is God unfolding for us?

_____

_____

Every believer is given a measure of faith. Faith can be as small as a mustard seed, and still be sufficient to level mountains in your life. Why? Applying faith over and over again will produce a mighty harvest. You do not have to feel "big" in faith to begin exercising it. Just as a runner who does not feel like a long-distance runner until he regularly exercises, so will your belief grow mighty when you sow and exercise your faith in the daily decisions of life.

What is the effect of sowing in faith? (Galatians 6:7)

_____

_____

Explain verse 8 in your own words.

_____

_____

_____

Walking in the flesh is walking in unbelief— having no faith in God. Sowing unbelief in our daily circumstances reaps corruption.

Read 2 Corinthians 9:6, 8-15. What occurs when you sow faith in God and His Word?

_____

_____

_____

How can we walk this way? Read Mark 4:20; Romans 10:17; and James 2:14-26. Intimacy with God is faith— unseen, deep, and eternal. How does faith begin and continue to increase? (Romans 10:17)

_____

_____

The Word of God is the seed of our faith. Faith will grow as the Word is planted in the heart. When a need arises in you, seek the truth in the Word concerning that need.

If you need peace, find every promise of God's peace in the Word. And saturate your heart and mind with what God says instead of what your circumstances say (2 Corinthians 4:18).

What is the process of reproducing faith? (Mark 4:20)

_____

_____

What do athletes or musicians enjoy doing?

_____

Well-trained athletes or accomplished musicians practice for hours, going over the fundamentals of their professions. Likewise, believers must spend time in the fundamentals of the faith— sowing truth in their hearts.

What else is needed to build your faith? (James 2:14-26)

_____

_____

True faith is expressed through our behavior. When we believe something to be true, we will act on it— not because our feelings or understanding, but because we *choose* to believe it.

COMPLETING OBEDIENCE

1)   Principle: Faith matures *only* as we exercise it by believing in a Sovereign God.

2)   Are you facing any impossible situations? What are they? Search God's Word and discover His promises to you concerning your needs.

3)   Take God at His Word, apply it to your heart and counter your feelings of unbelief.

4)   Memorize Romans 4:20-21.

THE STRENGTH OF PRAISE AND WORSHIP

"Shout joyfully to God, all the earth; Sing the glory of His name; Make His praise glorious."

Psalm 66:1-2

Focusing Your Heart

Worshipping You in spirit and truth, oh Lord, is the highest honor of life. With all of my heart and strength, I declare Your joy, glory, and worth today.

Fixing Your Mind

A life of praise will radiate from the believer who is intimately related with God. The Lord longs to have fellowship with one who worships Him in spirit and truth, uninhibited by the world. A lifestyle of sacrificing will produce deep joy and deliverance.

<u>FULFILLING HIS WILL</u>

A. The Heart of Praise and Worship

What is the nature of praise in the life of a believer? (Hebrews 13:15; Psalm 50:14,23)

_____

_____

Define sacrifice.

_____

_____

Why does God's Word describe praise as sacrifice?

_____

_____

A Theological Word Book of the Bible describes sacrifice in Hebrew culture with three underlying motives: 1) as a "gift to God"; 2) as a "means of entering into communion with God"; or 3) as a "means of releasing life, whether for the benefit of God Himself, or the worshipper". All of these require us to lose our own life and its cares in the presence of One infinitely greater and most worthy of glory and honor.

What challenges do Matthew and Paul give to those who profess Christ? (Matthew 16:24-26; Romans 12:1)

_____

_____

Read Psalm 40: 1-5, 8-10. Why was David overwhelmed with praise and adoration toward the Lord?

_____

_____

How does David admonish us to live? (Psalm 40:16)

_____

_____

The believer's life should declare the praises and glory of God. After David became consumed with God's presence and character, he quickly learned to respond with thanksgiving and awe. Those who desire intimacy with the Father, who are thankful for their deliverance from sin, self, and Satan, will be filled with continuous praise for God!

B. The Increase of Praise

Read John 3:30-31. Whose life was the greatest to John the Baptist?

_____

What great truth was he proclaiming through these simple words?

_____

_____

What was Paul's only reason for boasting? (Galatians 6:14)

_____

Read Jeremiah 9:23-24. Contrast the two examples of boasting and give your thoughts concerning the outcome of each.

_____

_____

_____

_____

The glory of God, Christ's sacrifice on the cross, and His mighty deeds are enough for our whole life to be filled with the utmost of praise, awe, and devotion. The realization of Jesus's exchange for our life causes us to live a life declaring Christ's increase and our decrease.

What is required in your heart to sincerely praise another? (Philippians 2:3-8)

_____

To bless the Lord continuously requires humility. The ego of man hates to exalt another. To center attention on God kills the flesh and strengthens the spirit. We commune with the spirit of God in our spirit, so when we praise Him, His life in us is built up (Matthew 26:41).

Paul's weakness and Christ's humility brought contentment and power. What were they able to overcome? (2 Corinthians 12:9-10; Philippians 2:9-11)

_____

_____

When we focus on God, we overcome the flesh and its passions and lusts because we no longer trust in ourselves. Read Psalm 50:19-23. The Psalmist is referring to one who misuses his tongue. What instruction is given to this kind of person? (v. 23)

_____

_____

The power of our tongue— when glorifying the Lord, when thanking Him— will set us free from our own destructive way and show us the path of deliverance.

C. Freedom to Adore

When expressing love to someone, how do you hope they will respond and speak to you? Really think about the question and describe it as specifically as possible.

_____

_____

_____

How are we to love God? (Matthew 22:37)

_____

David worshipped the Lord. How? (2 Samuel 6:5,14-22)

_____

_____

What sacrifice did David make for his unrestrained worship? (v. 16, 22)

_____

_____

What did he gain? (2 Samuel 7:12-16)

_____

_____

David learned to bless the Lord by spending hours with Him tending sheep on the hillside. He trusted in the faithfulness of the Lord to deliver him from the lion, the bear, Goliath, and Saul. He intimately knew the One worthy of his uninhibited joy and love. You, too, can experience God's power when you focus on Him, deny yourself, and discover the freedom only he can provide.

COMPLETING OBEDIENCE

1) Principle: True praise and worship strengthens the spirit and delivers the believer from waywardness.

2) What is hindering your praise and worship of God?

3) Read 2 Chronicles 20. Discover the power of praise over your enemy, the devil. What area of your life needs deliverance?

4) Memorize Hebrews 13:15.

GLORY IN THE SUFFERINGS

"For you have been called in this purpose, since Christ also suffered for you, leaving you an example for you to follow in his steps."

1 Peter 2:21

Focusing Your Heart

Lord, I want to know the deep things of Your heart. Knowing You means I must walk where You have walked. Lead me to experience the awesome power of Your resurrection life as I walk in the fellowship of Your sufferings.

Fixing Your Mind

Suffering is part of the journey toward maturity in Christ. It opens the way for God to give us His comfort, nurture His character in us, and allow us to share in Christ's glory.

FULFILLING HIS WILL

A. The Provision of Comfort

God allows suffering in our lives to bring about brokenness and total abandonment. During times of desperation, the Lord is able to rush in and comfort us beyond our comprehension when we submit to His will.

Recall a situation in your life when someone comforted you in a time of hurt or need. Describe the situation.

_____

_____

_____

Jesus desires to have a close and intimate relationship with us when we are suffering.

What two things are guaranteed to flow into our lives when we are united with Christ? (2 Corinthians 1:3-7)

1) _____

2) _____

What does verse 4 promise that we will be able to do after receiving this comfort?

_____

This is the same grace that strengthened Paul, enabling him to continue to share the gospel, even while suffering.

In John 11, the death of Lazarus caused great sorrow in his sisters, Martha and Mary. They sent the word to Jesus concerning their brother.

How did Martha, and later Mary, respond to the news of Jesus's arrival? (v. 20, 29)

_____

_____

_____

What was the first thing they told Jesus when they saw him? (v. 21, 32)

_____

_____

_____

Desperate for help, they ran to Jesus instead of relying on the comfort of those around them. They willingly exposed their desires, disappointments, and hurts before Him. Because they chose to be honest in the presence of the Lord, Jesus was able to interact with them about their need. How did He identify with them? (v. 33-35)

_____

_____

_____

When Martha and Mary turned to Jesus, it allowed Him to work in their situation with full authority. He was able to share in their pain and comfort them, meeting their greatest need. What did Jesus do because of their belief? (v.38-40)

_____

_____

_____

Martha and Mary experienced the resurrection life of Christ. The way we choose to respond to suffering births life or death. Coping with a tough situation in our own strength produces death. However, depending on Christ brings life and peace to the heart.

B. Suffering Produces Character

Paul suffered many trials that matured him in faith. He endured physical pain at the hand of men and nature, emotional pain in relationships, and spiritual pain as he agonized over those who God entrusted to him.

Identify the specific ways Paul suffered.

2 Corinthians 11:23-27

_____

2 Timothy 4:10

_____

2 Corinthians 11:28-29

_____

God uses suffering in our life to nurture His character in us. A believer's brokenness when suffering allows God to correct and instruct in His ways.

What word of encouragement is given to those who suffer? (Hebrews 12:6)

_____

_____

What is the result of God's discipline upon our lives? (Hebrews 12:10-11)

_____

_____

Read 1 Peter 5:10. After we have suffered, what will the Lord do for us?

_____

_____

God's plan to produce holiness in the lives of His children will be accomplished. He is aware of every pain, trial, and struggle we must endure as we become like His Son. Jesus also experienced suffering. What was the purpose of His pain? (Hebrews 5:8-9)

_____

_____

Since Jesus was never disobedient, why did He suffer?

_____

Obeying God will bring persecution from the world, accusations from the devil, and resistance from the flesh. The resultant suffering opens the door for us to enter into a dependence on God's character in us so that we can endure and overcome. Like Christ, we *learn* to become like God in our responses to the crisis of life.

What results from persevering in suffering? (Romans 5:3-5; James 1:2-4)

_____

We must embrace suffering in order to mature in Christ, knowing God our Father only allows trials which conform us to His image.

C. His Glory Revealed

Read 1 Peter 4:12-19. Why should the believer rejoice?

_____

Define glory.

_____

Glory is the fullness of God's character as it is revealed. Stephen and Jesus were two men who encountered the glory of God. In Acts 7, Stephen boldly preached the testimony of Jesus to the spiritual leaders of his day. Read Acts 7:54-60. What did Stephen experience in the midst of angry accusations?

_____

_____

What life Principle allowed Stephen to have joy even in his death? (John 12:23-26)

_____

_____

By willingly submitting his life, Stephen was able to see God in all His glory (Matthew 5:8).

Jesus also experienced God's glory. How is Jesus described in Hebrews 1:3?

_____

_____

Jesus not only saw the glory of God, He became His glory. As Christ surrendered His life to the will of the Father, the fullness of God's nature was revealed in Him.

1 Peter 4:14 says the spirit of glory and of God rests on those who suffer for Christ's sake. We also have the opportunity to receive God's glory into our lives. Read Romans 8:18. Where will the glory be revealed?

What can our present troubles achieve for us? (2 Corinthians 4:17)

"...just as He chose us in Him before the foundation of the world, that we should be holy and blameless before Him. In love He predestined us to adoption as sons through Jesus Christ to Himself, according to the kind intention of His will, to the praise of the glory of His grace, which He freely bestowed on us in the Beloved... to the end that we who were the first to hope in Christ should be the praise of His glory." (Ephesians 1:4-6, 12)

COMPLETING OBEDIENCE

1) Principle: Obedience to God is perfected in the midst of suffering.

2) We learn to become like God in our responses to the crisis of life. What difficult choices are you facing? Will you choose to respond in a Godly way?

3) Memorize Hebrews 5:8.

CHALLENGE 10

LOYALTY IN THE KINGDOM

"For I delight in loyalty rather than sacrifice, and in the knowledge of God rather than burnt offerings."

Hosea 6:6

Focusing Your Heart

Father, forgive me for having my own definition of loyalty in Your kingdom. As I am learning to hear Your heart, I will to love as You love.

Fixing Your Mind

Loyalty in God's kingdom is not determined by one's reputation or good deeds. It is a matter of faithfully loving God and others in the daily routine of life, putting them first.

FULFILLING HIS WILL

A. Rebellious Israel

Read Hosea 1-2:13. Summarize Israel's behavior in God's sight.

_____

_____

_____

_____

How did Israel become a harlot? (Hosea 2:7; 4:12)

_____

_____

What was His response to her harlotry? Be specific
(Hosea 2:3-13).

_____

_____

_____

Israel became a harlot by pursuing lovers other than
God. She offered sacrifice, celebrated feasts, sabbaths,
and worshipful assemblies, yet God condemned her as a
harlot. Read Isaiah 29:13; 30:9. How did God portray
rebellious Israel?

_____

_____

In what does God delight? (1 Samuel 15:22)

_____

_____

God's love is not based on performance. A form of
godliness can give the appearance of loyalty. However,
disloyalty is a matter of the heart, rooted in rebellion.
Fidelity in obeying the voice of the Lord is a definite
mark of intimacy with Him. He is grieved and withdraws
His presence over those who seek to find fulfillment in
other lovers.

B. Delighting in Loyalty

Explain Hosea 6:6 in your own words.

_____

_____

This truth lies at the heart of Jesus' struggle with the Pharisees and Sadducees. Read Matthew 9:9-13.

What was the Pharisees' specific problem with Jesus? (v. 11)

_____

_____

How does He answer them? (v. 12-13)

_____

_____

The Pharisees were most concerned with their reputation with appearing outwardly clean, untouched by sinners. In contrast, the compassion of God's heart loves those who are unlovely, and draws near to them.

Read Matthew 12:1-8. Write out the Pharisees' complaint against Jesus. (v. 1-2)

_____

_____

Give the life principle Jesus gives to them. (v. 3-8)

_____

_____

What truth is Jesus unfolding? (Isaiah 66:2)

_____

_____

"The intimacy of the Lord is for those who fear Him, and He will make them know His covenant." (Psalm 25:14)

C. Loyalty in the Kingdom

Loyalty to God will be demonstrated in our relationships to others. The integrity of our responses to life and those around us will be affected by the humility and obedience of our heart before God. How will our relationships reflect the faithfulness of our walk with God?

1) Proverbs 17:17

_____

_____

_____

2) Matthew 6:14-15

_____

_____

_____

3) Matthew 7:1-5, 12

_____

_____

_____

4) Ephesians 4:14-15, 29

_____

_____

_____

Read Galatians 5:22-26. Where does the fruit of the spirit reside?

_____

How does a person mature in the character of the spirit?

_____
_____
_____

The believer learns to be peaceful, patient, and kind through relationships.

Every conflict gives an opportunity for the believer to choose obedience to the spirit and loyalty to brothers and sisters in the kingdom. Failure to relate properly in human relationships diminishes the life and fruit of the spirit. Are your loyalties divided?

"Many a man proclaims his own loyalty, but who can find a trustworthy man?" (Proverbs 20:6)

COMPLETING OBEDIENCE

1) Principle: Godly loyalty to another reflects one's intimate commitment to Christ.

2) Are you pursuing lovers other than Christ? Why?

3) Have you been disloyal to another brother or sister? Repent and be reconciled.

4) Memorize Hosea 6:6.

ABOUT THE AUTHOR

Becky Castle

Becky Castle is the Founder and Executive Director of Cornelius Connection International, a ministry with the focus of equipping the Body of Christ to advance the Gospel, establish God's presence, and build Kingdom relationships. Becky also is the Founder and Executive Director of a ministry called the Exchange, a teaching and training on how to live a life empowered by our oneness with Christ through the Cross and Resurrection. Becky has studied and walked out the Word of God in a deep way impacting both her own life and the lives of others throughout her 45+ years of knowing Christ through student work, mission work, establishing and leading in churches, and especially through teaching and discipling others. Over the past 5 years Becky has been aligned with Chuck Pierce and Global Spheres, Inc. She is currently the leader of an apostolic center in Houston, TX called Launch Houston, and oversees the discipleship training school there, Teleios Institute. She has written several Bible Study books entitled "Challenges in Complete Obedience", a study in how to experience the fullness of God in our daily life.

MINISTRY AND AUTHOR
CONTACT INFORMATION

Becky Castle

Cornelius Connection International

2800 Antoine Dr. #2842

Houston, Tx 77092

www.corneliusconnection.net

www.launchhouston.org

**CORNELIUS
CONNECTION**
INTERNATIONAL

Series 1 **Embracing the Nature of Your Father God**
Series 2 **Experiencing the Depth of the Exchanged Life**
Series 3 **Captivated By the Love of Christ**
Series 4 **Dwelling Behind the Veil of Holiness**
Series 5 **Character of Christ Within**

Made in the USA
Columbia, SC
09 March 2024